Over Due

Freda Gardner

BookLeaf Publishing

India | USA | UK

Presentation by *BookLeaf Publishing*

Web: www.bookleafpub.com

E-mail: info@bookleafpub.com

ISBN: 9789363301801

First edition 2024

DEDICATION

I dedicate this book to my mama. Thank you for introducing me to   the love of how certain words can form into some the most powerful phrases that stick with us until the end of life. I love you and miss you .

Its Right Here

Now if my memory serves me right, It was the
4th of July
When I laid my eyes on you for the 1st time I
said this man has got to be mine
Then in a heartbeat love came to me
Rescued me from things the naked eye couldn't
see
I'm so grateful for him now I have a new love
Ill never let go why would I your love is the best
Ive know
But truthfully its not up to me
You know its here my love its here and Ill never
let go
I got me a new love its right here.

In My Mind

They don't make them like you no more
I aint never seen anything like you before
Skin like caramel brown eyes and I can tell
That you are sweet to the touch
All I need is one shot to show you what I can do
Dont you know that I really don't want nothing
from you
Just your love and that's all
In my mind In my mind
In my mind we are so good together
I want you
You don't have to do anything for me
Just show me you care
I want you

You Are

Dreams that I dream I pray to come true
God must have heard them because he sent me
you
Perfect to me in each and every way
Honest and pure that's what you are
You are all that I need and more
The reason I love you its so clear
So good to me
You are , you are.

Dreaming

Paradise, that's where I am when I think of you .
Feeling the sweetest feeling that I ever had when
I lay my eyes on you .
If I am sleep or if I am dreaming of you , don't
wake me.
Always miss the chance to feel your touch I
really want you that much, this much
If I am dreaming don't wake me.

I Love You More

Where did these feelings come from they snuck
up on me and now I'm sprung
Here is the tricky part do I tell you
I don't want to keep you in the dark but I don't
want to mess this up
I love you more
I love you more than you know
Please stay with me you are my joy
I love you more than you know

I Am His

This love that we share is so beautiful so perfect
to me
Never have to doubt his love for me
I am his and he is mine.
This love cannot be taken from us
He is my heart
 I am his and he is mine

Always

The stars shine so bright at night
Just like my love for you ,
It will last for all time

This love will stay with me for always
Whatever you do don't take it away
Oceans and seas cannot part me from you
Whatever you do know this I will stay true

Come Back To Me

If I gave you the moon
Or maybe the stars
Even the ocean or the sea
Would that help you bring me back to me

Who do I believe

Who do I believe
Who do I trust
When you never did me wrong but all the facts
are starting to add up
But in your case you never lied to me so why
would you start now
It doesn't add up to me
Who do I believe

Nothing Here For Me

Started to see the light when I spend valentines
night
All alone waiting and home but you never
showed
What am I to do , you are not the man that I
thought you were

Whatever we had is gone and what is gone we
had
I have to cut my loses and move on got to do
this for me because nothing is here no more .

Love no one else

You were my passion , you were my soul
Had my love all wrapped up all ready to go
Filling my head up with the thoughts of new
love
When I was just some one to pass the time with
nothing else
Had my eyes dancing with the thought of being
with someone like you
All of this was so brand new
Just the thought of having someone to call my
own
Blocked my vision of seeing what was really
going on
But I don't want to love no one else but you
I cant live with out you I already tried
I don't want to love no one else

Runaway

I'm asking myself should I even stop trying with
you , I know that you don't want me.
I guess I misread the feelings that I thought you
had for me
Maybe I was seeing what I wanted to see Now
my tears have my eyes blinded I cannot see
All I want to know why is why didn't want want
me . Why did you have to runaway
Runaway from me
Dont you know that I need your love
Why did you runway from me
Please come back to me

I Know

I don't want to be sad for the rest of my life
So that's why I gotta cut these ties with you
But I know , I know that I will be better off
without you
All you did was cause me hurt and pain that I
know I didn't need in my life
I know that I am so much better with out you
I don't need you so just go far away

I Dont Want To Cry

In the mist of my heart break
In the mist of heart ache
I'm praying dear Lord don't let a tear roll down
my face
I need to tell myself that I will make and I can
be strong
I have to hold on
I just don't wanna cry

I Thought It Was Over

Treated me like I was nothing at all
And then when ended it was all my fault
I swore I would lock up all these feelings
And through away the key
Somehow the snuck back up on me
The feelings that I have for you
But I keep telling myself no

I thought it was over my feelings for you are
gone
Cant keep crying wishing you were here
Got to get a hold of me I'm not acting right
I thought it was over

I tried

You know I loved you and I would have done
anything for you
But you didn't want me
You didn't want me no more
I tried so hard but I never could get through to
you
I tried to tell myself its over

Emotions

Emotions , you got me feeling them
Got me tripping over you , got my words tangled
its true
I swear that I see you when I'm sleeping your
brown eyes they haunt me
They awake me and take me far away
This is what you do to me I get emotions

Close My Eyes

It was always a necessary thing
For us to be together
We went together like butter and bread
But some things got me questioning this
How you gonna leave me standing hear
When I'm suppose to be your main girl
You tell me that you want nothing to do with me
Calling me telling me its over
How could you be this cold hearted
When you gave me your word I was the one for
you
I wont play the sheltered victim anymore
Dont even bother me anymore
I close my eyes so when I wake up
I can see things better
Thats why I close my eyes
I can look back and see what you did
Maybe its better this way I knew something was
wrong
And I know something isn't right that's why I
close my eyes
Because when I wake up

www.ingramcontent.com/pod-product-compliance
Lightning Source LLC
LaVergne TN
LVHW050312210726
843507LV00020B/3109